T

RELIGION

OF

THE FORCE

REVISED, SECOND EDITION

THE
RELIGION
OF
THE FORCE

REVISED, SECOND EDITION

Richard G. Howe
and
Norman L. Geisler

Bastion Books

Matthews, North Carolina

The Religion of the Force, Revised, Second Edition
by Richard G. Howe and Norman L. Geisler

Copyright © 1983, 2015 Norman L. Geisler. All rights reserved.

Published by Bastion Books | P.O. Box 1033 | Matthews, NC 28106 |
USA
www.bastionbooks.com

Printed in the United States of America

ISBN–13: 978-1533324955
ISBN–10: 1533324956

The first edition of *The Religion of the Force* was authored by Norman
Geisler and J. Yutaka Amano and published in 1983 by Quest Publi-
cations. This second edition was updated and revised by Richard G.
Howe and Norman Geisler in 2015. The cover art and desktop publish-
ing were courtesy of Christopher T. Haun. The "How to Know God"
appendix was written by Christopher Haun and Norman Geisler.

CONTENTS

Star Wars is one of the greatest phenomena of our times. Few are aware that this great saga has great religious implications in it. From beginning to end *Star Wars* creates a religion for our times. It is a religion that centers on "the Force," a term for a mostly pantheistic conception of God.[1] The Force permeates the plots, themes, and chief characters of all the Star Wars stories.

Many of the characters in the movies attest to the religious nature of the films. Moff Tarkin considered devotion to the Force to be the "religion" of the Jedi. Admiral Motti's referred to the Force as being as both sorcery and an "ancient religion." Han Solo referred to it a "hokey religion" that relies on antiquated weapons.

George Lucas, the creator of the series, confesses that it reflects his own religious beliefs. In an interview he also made it clear that,

> When I did *Star Wars* I consciously set about to re–create myths and the classic mythological motifs and I wanted to use those motifs to deal with issues that existed today.

He also was quite direct concerning his intentions for the Force:

> I put the Force into the movies in order to try to awaken a certain kind of spirituality in young people—more a

belief in God than a belief in any particular religious system.

Further he says,

[The Force] is designed primarily to make young people think about the mystery....Think about this for a second. Is there a God? What does God look like? What does God sound like? What does God feel like? How do we relate to God?

Of course, there are distinct differences between "the Force" and "God" as conceived in Western religions like Judaism and Christianity (see chap. 3), but this is precisely the point. The Force is not a theistic conception of God, and it should not be taken as such. And despite any similarities, it cannot serve as a Christian allegory. But it is religious, and no one should be deceived into thinking otherwise (see chapter 2). Indeed, *Star Wars* is an all–encompassing religion which has captured the minds and hearts of millions of people, both young and old. And it will serve to replace Christianity in the minds of millions. This, from a Christian perspective, presents one of the great challenges to the orthodox Christian faith in our time.

"Prepare to meet the Force."
—Darth Vader

The *Star Wars* phenomena has shaped the ways a lot of us think and talk about our world, if not our reality. The saga began in 1977 with *Star Wars: A New Hope*. This inaugural movie was actually episode IV. Prequels came out later to fill us in on the background stories and to set the stage for taking the story forward.

Lucas followed up in 1980 with episode V, *The Empire Strikes Back* and in 1983 with episode VI, *Return of the Jedi.* After a hiatus, *The Phantom Menace* exploded onto the screen in 1999. Such was the sensation that the April 26, 1999 edition of *Time* had a cover story on the event. Then, in three–year increments like the first releases, *The Phantom Menace* was followed in 2002 by *Attack of the Clones* and in 2005 by *Revenge of the Sith.* No doubt that the newest releases raised as many questions as they answered regarding the exploits of the characters. Just as rumors floated around about whether any prequels would actually see the light of day, for many years the rumors floated around even after the six movies as to whether the story was really finished.

At the time of this writing, the seventh installment, *Star Wars: The Force Awakens*, remains shrouded in secrecy and the director of the eighth and final episode has just been announced. We can only assume that what we say here about the first six episodes of the saga will also apply to the last two.

There are many things to say in praise of the whole *Star Wars* phenomenon. To bring to the screen even a fraction of what he saw in his own imagination, Lucas had to create a new production company with new photographic and special effects techniques. While they were being developed, the techniques had to be kept quite secret. "Part of this secrecy" [before the release of *Star Wars Episode IV: A New Hope*] was "designed to protect the innovative special effects work."[2] The production of the first *Star Wars* movie required the founding of Lucas's special effects division of his Lucas film production company: Industrial Light & Magic (ILM). ILM is considered "one of the preeminent visual effects firms in the industry."[3] According to their website, ILM realized that "in order to achieve the epic space battles called for in *Star Wars: Episode 4, A New Hope* a new approach to filming miniatures had to be developed. Traditional techniques simply would not work for filming the elaborate dogfights Director George Lucas had envisioned."[4] Thus, the team,

> . . . led by John Dykstra ... developed a camera system that could be controlled by custom–designed, hard–wired electronics and thus record and replicate exacting camera movements time and time again . . . [which] utilized a camera mounted to a crane arm, which in turn

rode on a dolly track. . . . [It] represented the first in a
long line of motion control cameras developed at ILM.[5]

Not only has *Star Wars* produced innovative techno-
logical breakthroughs, but in a real way (despite the crit-
icisms we shall bring to bear later on), these movies have
conveyed some innovations on important moral points.
There is more to life than just the physical. There is a battle between good and evil. There is virtue in cooperation
for the common good over against a selfish pursuit of one's
own interests. As Lucas explained to journalist Bill Moyers,

> I think the core issues that I'm dealing with are—if they
> were valid 2,000 years ago, they've got to still be valid
> today, even though they're not in fashion. ... The im-
> portance of, say, friendship and loyalty... are very, very
> important to the way we live our lives.[6]

There certainly is very little to gainsay Lucas here and
on perhaps certain other specific points. While acknowl-
edging, however, these virtues, it is incumbent upon us
that we recognize more fully what the exact message of
Star Wars is.

Two main points shall occupy our analysis. First, we
shall establish that there is a "religion" of the Force. Second, we will compare (note its similarities) and contrast
(note its differences) this religion of the Force with Christianity. Count me (Richard) among the biggest fans of the
series. I even liked Jar Jar Binks! Thus, nothing we say
ought to be construed as an attack on the artistic genius of
George Lucas and his masterful works.

2 | IS THERE A RELIGION OF THE FORCE?

> "The Jedi are extinct.... You, my friend,
> are all that's left of their religion."
> —The Grand Moff Tarkin

We suspect that some might be skeptical that *Star Wars* is religious in any sense. Perhaps, the critic might say, we are reading too much into the dialogue and symbolism. But what did George Lucas himself have to say about what he was trying to do with *Star Wars*? "When I did Star Wars I consciously set about to re–create myths and the classic mythological motifs and I wanted to use those motifs to deal with issues that existed today."[7] Lucas will have more to say about how he understood his own project and exactly what message he was trying to convey. As for the movies themselves, what do we find about its religious nature and message?

Jedi Ways Are Called a Religion

Is there, indeed, a "religion" of the Force? It is explicitly referred to as a religion in the movies. With skepticism and contempt in his voice, Admiral Motti, in *A New Hope*, sneers at Vader, "Don't try to frighten us with your sorcerer's ways, Lord Vader. Your sad devotion to that ancient religion has not helped you conjure up the stolen data tapes or given you clairvoyance enough to find the Rebel's hidden fort…"[8] with his words cut short by Darth Vader's Force choke. Vader then retorts "I find your lack of faith disturbing"[9] again pointing to the religious nature of the Force.

Watching from the sidelines as Obi Wan begins to inaugurate Luke into the ways of the Force, Han Solo advises Luke "Hokey religions and ancient weapons are no match for a good blaster at your side, kid."[10] Last, while these two specific references to the Force being a religion might be discounted as the dismissive observations of unbelievers, the words of Grand Moff Tarkin have a ring of subtle respect if not regretful sadness when he observes, "The Jedi are extinct. You, my friend, are all that's left of their religion."[11]

George Lucas himself recognized, indeed, intended, this religious aspect of his project. He told Bill Moyers,

> There's, again, a mixture of all kinds of mythology and religious beliefs that have been amalgamated into the movie, and I've tried to take the ideas that seem to cut across the most cultures, because I'm fascinated by that and I think that's one of the things that I really got from Joe Campbell, was that what he was trying to do is find the common threads through the various mythology, through the religions.[12]

Even more to the point he said,

> When the film came out, almost every single religion took *Star Wars* and used it as an example of their reli-

gion … If it's a tool that can be used to make old stories be new and relate to younger people, that's what the whole point was.[13]

Further evidence that the Force is a religion is that it requires "faith" in order to work. We have already seen that Vader himself recognizes that it takes "faith" to use the Force when he expressed his being disturbed at Admiral Motti's lack thereof. Vader's words are deliberate on the part of Lucas. In an interview with Moyers, we find this exchange. Moyers asked "Ultimately, doesn't it take, particularly in religion, a leap of faith? Kierkegaard's leap of faith?"

Lucas responded,

Yes. Yes. Definitely. You'll notice Luke uses that quite a bit through the films. Not to rely on his senses, not to rely on the computers, but to rely on faith. That is what 'Use the Force' is. It is a leap of faith [to believe] that there are mysteries and powers larger than we are, and that you have to trust your feelings in order access these things.[14]

Even still, Lucas's notion of faith is less a notion of trust as it is a sort of "power of positive thinking." One's ability to wield the Force depends upon one's degree of confidence that the mind can affect physical reality. This is vividly displayed in *The Empire Strikes Back* when Luke tries to levitate his ship out of swamp on Dagobah. When Luke sees the ship sink even deeper into the water, he exclaims "Oh no. We'll never get it out now!"

Yoda responds, "So certain are you?"

Then, with an exhale of exasperation he observes, "Always with you it cannot be done. Hear you nothing that I say?" In his own defense, Luke argues, "Master, moving stones around is one thing" which he had been doing with a certain level of success. Then, gesturing toward the sunken ship he continues, "But this is totally different!"

Yoda, not giving up despite the hard–headedness of his pupil, presses, "No. No different. Only different in your mind." Even here, we begin to see that the notion of "faith" has more to do with the power and attitude of the mind. "You must unlearn what you have learned," Yoda concludes.

Willing to take on the seemingly impossible task, Luke gives in, "Alright, I'll give it a try."

"No!" Yoda interrupts. "Try not. Do! Or do not. There is no try."

Disappointedly, Luke can get only so far with his ability in the Force before he is exhausted and the ship, which he managed to partially levitate out, sinks back down and disappears below the water's surface. Yoda bows his head in disappointment. Breathing heavily, Luke admits to Yoda, "I can't. It's too big!"

Yoda seizes the moment for an object lesson. "Size matters not," meaning, as it will become evident in a moment that neither the Jedi's size nor the size of the object of the Force matters. Yoda continues, "Look at me. Judge me by my size do you? Hum? And well you should not." He then explains that, because the Force surrounds everything and is even between all things, including between the land and the sunken ship.

Luke, realizing what Yoda is getting at, conveys his unbelief, "You want the impossible," and walks away. Luke now poised to witness the display of the Force's power when Yoda, as small has he is, is able to levitate the ship and place it on dry land. Then comes the climax to the entire scene. Luke is astounded by what he has just seen and says, "I don't believe it!"

To which Yoda responses, "That is why you failed."

Thus, we are to conclude that if Luke had only believed that he could do it, he would have done it. It is only because he doubted that he was impotent to utilize the Force to a sufficient degree. These references to the Jedi "religion" by name and Lucas's own words leave no doubt that the Jedi use of the Force was presented as a religion in the *Star Wars* series.

The Force Mirrors Religion

Supreme Being

Not only is the Jedi use of the Force called a religion three times in Star Wars, but the Jedi beliefs mirror religion. The Force mimics a Supreme Being. To be sure, Lucas discounted the notion that the Force was God. Admitting that his movies would be "a thin base for theology"[15] he cautioned "that's why I would hesitate to call the Force God." Despite his wanting to minimize the connection, there are too many aspects of the Force that suggest the notion of God to be ignored.

The Force is omnipresent and grounds the universe.[16] Obi Wan explained it to Luke this way: "The Force is what gives a Jedi his power. It's an energy field created by all living things. It surrounds us, penetrates us. It binds the galaxy together."[17] Yoda concurs. "My ally is the Force. And a powerful ally it is. Life creates it. Makes it grow. Its energy surrounds us and binds us."[18] It is evident that there are stark contrasts between the Force and the God of Christianity. But we will save our look at those differences for a little later.

Spirituality

There is dominant element of spirituality in *Star Wars*. Lucas was quite direct concerning his intentions for the Force. "I put the Force into the movies in order to try to awaken a certain kind of spirituality in young people— more a belief in God than a belief in any particular religious system."[19] Further he says,

> [The Force] is designed primarily to make young people think about the mystery. Not to say 'Here's the answer.' It's to say 'Think about this for a second. Is there a God? What does God look like? What does God sound

like? What does God feel like? How do we relate to God?'[20]

While Lucas claimed that he did not "see *Star War* as profoundly religious," he did see it as,

> . . . taking all of the issues that religion represents and trying to distill them down into a more modern and more easily accessible construct that people can grab onto to accept the fact that there is a greater mystery out there. When I was ten years old I asked my mother I said 'Well, if there's only one God, why are there so many religions?' And over the years I've been pondering that question ever since and it would seem to me that the conclusion I've come to is that all the religions are true. They just see a different part of the elephant."[21]

Perhaps Lucas was only humbly saying that it was not profound. He certainly could not have meant that it was in no sense religious.

Morality

We have already seen a degree to which *Star Wars* involved the struggle of morality. Just as religion does, it aims toward the "good" which is achievable by engaging the light side of the Force. It also acknowledges the moral

fallenness of humans. In explaining the character of Darth
Maul, Lucas says "This one is all human. I wanted him
to be like an alien but I wanted him to be human enough
that we could identify with him because he's not sort of a
monster we can't identify with."

Bill Moyers then correctly interjects "He's us."

To which Lucas responds "Yeah, he's the evil within
us."[22] More to the point Lucas summarizes, "The film is
ultimately about the dark side and the light side, and those
sides are designed around compassion and greed, and we
all have those two sides of us, and that we have to make
sure that those two sides of us are in balance."[23]

Seemingly Supernatural "Miracles"

Through the Force, the Jedi can perform seemingly supernatural "miracles." For example, in *The Empire Strikes
Back*, we see Luke attempt and then Yoda succeed at levi-
tating Luke's ship out of the swamp on Dagobah. In *Attack
of the Clones* the adult Anakin levitates a piece of fruit
from Padme's plate to his own, cuts a slice, and levitates
the slice back to Padme's plate. In several of the films, the
Jedi use the power of the Force to retrieve their out–of–
reach light sabers. The Force also enabled the Jedi to see
the future, a feat usually only possible in most religions by
means of the power of God.

While training Luke in the ways of the Force, Yoda
soothingly intones "Through the Force, things you will

see: other places, the future, the past, old friends long gone."[24] And if Chancellor Palatine is to be believed, the Dark Lord of the Sith, Darth Plagueis the Wise, was even able to use the Force to influence the midi–chlorians (the intelligent, microscopic life forms that live symbiotically inside the cells of other life forms) to create life and to keep those he cared about from dying.[25] It turns out that there is every reason to believe what Palatine is saying in as much as Yoda much later on tacitly implies this possibility. When he reveals to Luke that he is about to die, Luke protests "Master Yoda, you can't die!" In response, Yoda says, "Strong am I with the Force—but not that strong."[26]

Life After Death

Just as in religion, you also find a notion of life after death. In *A New Hope*, Obi Wan dies and leaves Luke feeling all alone in the task that lies before him. In *The Empire Strikes Back* when Luke is expressing his discouragement to R2D2, he hears the comforting words "Yoda will always be with you" from none other than Obi Wan who has returned in "ghostly" form to offer Luke a bit more counseling as a "spirit guide" if you will.[27] At the triumphant end of *Return of the Jedi*, during the celebration on the forest moon of Endor, Luke pensively looks off into the woods. The scene pans to what he is seeing, and there we encounter a (clearly deliberate) "trinity"—Anakin Skywalker, Obi Wan Kenobi, and Yoda all with a transparent shimmering in an "other worldly" manner, smiling approvingly on all that has finally taken place.

The Mimicking of Christian Doctrines

Other elements mimic Christianity in particular. Throughout the movies (one website noted eighteen times) there is some form or another of the salutation "May the Force be with you"—an obvious play on the departing words of Jesus Christ when he said to His disciples in Matt. 28:20 "Lo, I am with you, always."

What is more, in *The Phantom Menace*, we encounter a not–so–cryptic hint to a virgin birth—a clear reference to the central Christian doctrine. Qui–Gon Jinn, who has been waxing more impressed with what he sees in the young Anakin Skywalker, asks his mother Shmi who his father is. Her response is puzzling if not startling. "There was no father. I carried him. I gave birth. I raised him. I can't explain what happened."[28]

We discover very soon, as Qui–Gon speculates before the Jedi Council, that Anakin might have been "conceived by the midi–chlorians." Might one speculate at the whether the midi–chlorians emulate the work of the Holy Spirit? Not only are they seemingly responsible for the conception of Anakin Skywalker, and that they "indwell" at least the Jedi (or soon–to–be Jedi), but Qui–Gon teaches young Anakin that "without the midi–chlorians life could not exist and we would have no knowledge of the Force" since they "continually speak to us, telling us the will of the

Force." He then encourages Anakin, "when you've learned to quiet your mind, you'll hear them speaking to you."[29]

In summary, many of the elements of traditional religious belief are found in the religion of the Jedi. George Lucas's biographer Dale Pollock put it bluntly: "The message of Star Wars is religious: God isn't dead, he's there if you want him to be. 'The laws really are in yourself,' Lucas is fond of saying; the Force dwells within."[30]

3 | WHAT IS GEORGE LUCAS'S RELIGION?

> **"For my ally is the Force.**
> **And a powerful ally it is."**
> **—Yoda**

It is clear that the Jedi have a religion, but is it the same as the religion of George Lucas, the writer of Star Wars? What are Lucas's religious beliefs?

Religious Influences

George Lucas had a nominal Methodist background with some exposure to a German Lutheran housekeeper. But George loathed this piety and resented Sunday School.[31] On July 4, 1981 a Lucas time capsule filled with memorabilia was placed in the cornerstone of the main house at Skywalker Ranch. In the black cylinder was also placed a small button which expresses Lucas's belief. On it were two words: "Question Authority."[32] This was typical of Lucas's attitude toward traditional Christian religion.

When Lucas was only six years of age he had a mystical experience. In his own words, "It centered around God, what is God, but more than that, what is reality?" George admits "It was very profound to me at the time." In fact it made a lasting impression on him about the mysteries of life.[33] When asked what his life is about, Lucas replied, "I am simply trying to struggle through life; trying to do God's bidding."[34]

Surviving a bad auto accident added to Lucas's sense of divine destiny. He believes that one cannot have that kind of experience without feeling that there is a reason for their being here on earth.[35] Such experiences gave Lucas a kind of fatalism about life. Even his great success is taken in this light. For he accepted that it happened and felt there was not much he could do about it. He felt it was just part of his fate.[36]

Admittedly Religious

Lucas does not deny that Star Wars is an expression of his own moral and religious beliefs. He told Time magazine, "There's more of me in Star Wars than I care to admit." Lucas confessed he was trying to say "that there is a God and there is both a good side and a bad side. You have a choice between them, but the world works better if you're on the good side."[37]

Lucas spoke of his Star Wars saga as a religious "fairy tale." He said, "It's where religion came from." They are "designed to teach man the right way to live and to give a moral anchor."[38]

George Lucas looks at the films as "a modern morality play, a psychological tool that children can use to understand the world better and their place in it and how to adjust to that."[39] Lucas does not blush at the thought of presenting a religious and moral message in Star Wars. In fact, he believes TV is valueless or amoral and desires to fill this void by the moral message of his movies.

Lucas prefers a film which imparts real values for living but by means of a larger–than–life dramatization.[40] He believes everyone is forgetting to tell children what is right and what is wrong. The Lucas biography admits Lucas "was imposing his values on the rest of the world, but he felt they were the right values."[41]

In brief, Lucas has deep religious and moral convictions which he desires to express to the children of our day who seem to him to be value free and religiously rootless. Hence, he wishes to create a modern religious myth by which young people can be taught the basic message about God, good and evil, and death. Few who have seen the dramatic way in which the Star Wars trilogy conveys Lucas's message can doubt the success of his efforts.

A biography on Lucas, *Skywalking*, frankly acknowledges that "Lucas wanted to instill in children a belief in a supreme being … a universal deity that he named the Force, a cosmic energy source that incorporates and consumes all living things."[42] Hence, the message of Star Wars is religious. God is alive for all who wish to believe.

For those who think Star Wars is simply entertainment, Newsweek responded pointedly, "People can croak,

'Entertainment! Entertainment!' until they're blue in the face. The fact remains that films like … 'Star Wars' have become jerry–built substitutes for the great myths and rituals of belief, hope and redemption that cultures used to shape before mass secular society took over."[43]

> **"The gospel according to Luke**
> **and the gospel according to Lucas**
> **would seem to be virtually the same."**
> **—Robert Short**

Is Star Wars a Christian Allegory?

While more can be said, perhaps this will suffice to show that, indeed, *Star Wars* is, in a very real sense, a religious movie. Seeing the evident religious message of Star Wars, some have concluded that it is a kind of Christian allegory. Robert Short, the author of *The Gospel from Outer Space*, told reporters, "In Star Wars, you have 'force'—a strong witness to the power of God." And the movie's greeting, 'May the force be with you,' is 'May the Lord be with you.' It is God's control."[44]

According to Short, this kind of story is also the good news of the Christian message, a message which proclaims that God has already triumphed over all of the forces of sin, evil, and death. So this victory has been totally accomplished for all people. "Therefore the gospel according to Luke and the gospel according to Lucas would seem to be virtually the same."[45]

Short believes that if the church would present the Christian message in the same way space movies have, then people would be lined up in the same record–breaking numbers at the church doors.

Similarities

Most of the similarities have already been mentioned in as much as they arise from the fact that, in a broad sense, Christianity is a religion as well. Being both religious, it is to be expected that there would be common themes between *Star Wars* and Christianity. Let it suffice to list a few. Both understand that there is a spiritual dimension to life. They both recognize that there is a supreme Power in the universe. They see mankind as caught in a conflict between good and evil and that he has a choice in this conflict. They both maintain that evil can be overcome by making proper contact with the Supreme Power, that faith is an essential ingredient in this contact with the Supreme Power, and that there is a glorious destiny (immortality) awaiting the faithful.

Are All Religions Basically the Same at the Core?

No doubt some will suggest that all this shows that the religion of the Force and Christianity are saying the same things at their core; as, indeed, all religions do according to the conventional wisdom. This apparent commonality among religions is what makes Lucas (as we have already seen) come to the conclusion that "all the religions are true. They just see a different part of the elephant."[46] This latter part accounts for all the apparent conflicts in the various religions. Thus, the conventional view says, all religions are the same at the core. They just differ on the peripherals.

However, upon closer examination, one finds that it is exactly the reverse. All religions are radically different in their core beliefs. But they are very similar in their peripheral beliefs. One should note the pattern.

Most of the world's religions and philosophies agree in the broad moral areas. In the East, Confucius said,

> What are the things that men consider right? Kindness on the part of the father, and filial duty on that of the son; gentleness on part of the elder brother, and obedience on that of the younger; righteousness on the part of the husband, and submission on that of the wife; kindness on the part of elders, and deference on that of juniors; with benevolence on the part of the ruler, and loyalty on that of the minister; —these ten are the things which men consider to be right."[47]

Wisdom from Hinduism tells us "Utter not a word by which anyone could be wounded," and "A sacrifice is obliterated by a lie and the merits of alms by an act of fraud," and "One should never strike a woman, not even with a flower." Buddhism teaches, "Supporting one's father and mother, cherishing wife and children and a peaceful occupation; this is the greatest blessings."[48] Many more examples could be marshaled to show that these broad themes of human interaction all follow a pattern. This has been recognized in the West as "Natural Law." This harmony here between the imperatives of Eastern and Western moral philosophers is no surprise to Bible believers. The Apostle Paul explains,

> For when Gentiles, who do not have the law, by nature
> do the things in the law, these, although not having the
> law, are a law to themselves, who show the work of the
> law written in their hearts, their conscience also bearing
> witness, and between themselves their thoughts accus-
> ing or else excusing them.[49]

In contrast to this wide unanimity, when one asks the question about the issues that define the various world religions, we see a very different picture.[50] On many of these question, there is very little agreement. In other words, while some variant of "Love your neighbor" might be held by all the world's religions, such a mandate is not a *defining* element of those religions. Christianity does indeed teach that we are to love our neighbor. But this is not the core of Christianity. Instead, it is an implication of the core. The core of any given religion must be sought in how they answer certain objective facts about reality, like "Does God exist?"; "What is God like?"; "Who is Jesus?"; "Is there life after death?"; "How does one gain eternal life or salvation or deliverance?"

When asking these types of questions, we find very little agreement. Whereas Theravada Buddhism has no God, various schools of Mahayana Buddhism (e.g., Tibetan Buddhism) have many gods. While early Vedic Hinduism was very nearly monotheistic, later Upanishadic Hinduism is pantheistic (all is God) and Bhakti Hinduism is polytheistic (many gods). Confucius's teachings contain no gods, no religious worship, and no revelations. Judaism, Islam,

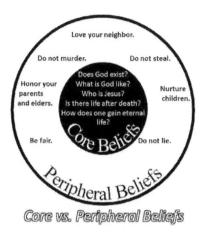

Do not murder.

Love your neighbor.

Do not steal.

Honor your parents and elders.

Does God exist?
What is God like?
Who is Jesus?
Is there life after death?
How does one gain eternal life?

Nurture children.

Be fair.

Core Beliefs

Do not lie.

Peripheral Beliefs

Core vs. Peripheral Beliefs

and Christianity maintains that there is only one God.

As far as God's nature is concerned, the gods of Tibetan Buddhism are angelic and demonic beings. Early Vedic Hinduism saw God as the "father of heaven." Later Upanishadic Hinduism saw God as the All. The Gods of Bhakti Hinduism are finite. Confucianism being atheistic, there is nothing for God to be like. In Judaism, the one, true God created the heavens and the Earth and revealed Himself to Abraham and Moses (which Christianity accepts). In Islam, the one true God created the heavens and the Earth and revealed Himself to many prophets, the last of whom was Mohammed (which Judaism and Christianity reject). In Christianity, there is only one God who is a Trinity of three persons (Father, Son, and Holy Spirit).

Regarding Jesus, some Buddhist see Jesus as one among many "enlightened ones," or Buddhas. In Bhakti Hinduism, Jesus is one of virtually countless "gods" to whom one can attach himself in devotion for "salvation." Given that there is no God in Confucianism, Jesus is nothing more than a man. Judaism sees Jesus as a well–intentioned (if misguided or misunderstood) Jewish rabbi but was not the promised Messiah of Israel. In Islam, Jesus is one of the greatest prophets (born of a virgin and a miracle worker) but he did not die on the cross or resurrect from the dead. Christianity knows Jesus is the unique Son of God (God in the flesh) who died for the sins of the world.

For life after death, Theravada Buddhism seeks to lead one to Nirvana which is extinction of desire. Pure Land Buddhism seeks to lead one to a heaven. The Hindu afterlife (deliverance from reincarnation) varies from absorption into the pantheistic God to a paradise of delights. Confucius's emphasis was on the ordering of society in this life. He avoided speculating about any afterlife. Modern Judaism focuses on the life that one lives in the here and now. In Islam, heaven awaits those who are counted worthy by Allah. Hell awaits all infidels and those on whom Allah's favor does not fall. In Christianity, heaven awaits all who believe the Gospel of Jesus. Hell awaits all unbelievers.

Last, what about how one gains eternal life? In Theravada Buddhism, Nirvana is by the Eight–fold path. In Pure Land Buddhism one finds heaven by the favor of Amida Buddah. In Hinduism, one must break the cycle of reincarnation by working off one's Karma. There is no afterlife to

attain in Confucianism. For modern Judaism, there is little
to no emphasis on any kind of afterlife. Islam teaches that
heaven is gained by service to Allah. Only a few can have
any assurance of avoiding hell. In Christianity, eternal life
is a gift that cannot be earned. It comes to those who trust
God's provision in Jesus.

Differences

Now that we are prepared to acknowledge that not all
religions are the same, we are in a position of recognize
the vast differences between the religion of the Force and
Christianity.

The Force vs. God

In *Star Wars*, The Force is an impersonal energy field,
created by living things and permeating all things.[51] We
have already seen both Obi Wan's and Yoda's teaching to
Luke on the nature of the Force. Obi Wan tells him "The
Force is what gives a Jedi his power. It's an energy field
created by all living things. It surrounds us, penetrates us.
It binds the galaxy together."[52]

Yoda concurs, "My ally is the Force. And a powerful
ally it is. Life creates it. Makes it grow. Its energy surrounds us and binds us."[53]

In contrast to the Force, Christianity understands God
as a personal being who is the transcendent Creator and
upholder of all things whose will for everyone is to have a

personal relationship with Him. Further, God has not left it to our own devices to find that relationship but has provided the reconciliation to Himself that we all need through the cross of Jesus Christ. (Matt. 6:9; John 14:9; Gen. 1:1, 21; Isaiah 40; Rom. 4:4–5; 2 Cor. 5:21.)

Good and Evil

In *Star Wars*, the Force has both a good side and an evil side. During Yoda's training of Luke we learn:

> A Jedi's strength flow from the Force. But beware of the Dark Side—anger, fear, aggression: the Dark Side of the Force are they. Easily they flow. Quick to join you in a fight. If once you start down the dark path, forever will it dominate your destiny. Consume you it will as it did Obi Wan's apprentice.[54]

The notion that there is a single reality or force or energy that is comprised of both good and evil is reminiscent of the eastern concept of Yin and Yang—a view that sees reality as being driven by the dynamic interaction and balance of opposites.[55] According to this view, "the whole world consists of two opposing yet complementary forces, yin and yang, which are optimally in perfect balance with each other on the whole."[56] In the theory Yin is passive, earth–related, cold, moist, mysterious, dark, and feminine while Yang is active, sky–related, hot, dry, clear, light, masculine. Even the notion of sweet and sour in Chinese cuisine arises from this world view. What is key here is the notion of balance. The individual elements complement each other. Thus, the idea of balance does not mean that these elements are blended to the point that their respective differences go away. Instead, the universe seeks a proper balance on the whole.

We find that the notion of balance plays a key role in *Star Wars*. A theme running through episodes I–III is that Anakin Skywalker is the chosen one who is to bring balance to the Force. After informing the Jedi Council about their encounter with what he is convinced is a Sith Lord, Qui–Gon Jinn lingers to fill them in on some even more significant news about his encounter with a most gifted young Anakin Skywalker. Yoda inquires, "Master Qui–Gon, more to say have you?"

Qui–Gon measuredly reveals "With your permission, my master: I've encountered a vergence in the Force."

Yoda, realizing the potential gravity of the news repeats his words "A vergence, you say."

Mace Windu, also realizing the implications of this turn of events asks "Located around a person?"

Qui–Gon continues, "A boy. His cells have the highest concentration of midi–clorians I have seen in a life form. It is possible he was conceived by the midi–clorians."

Mace Windu then attempts to jump to the chase regarding what Qui–Gon is hinting at. "You refer to the prophecy of the one who will bring balance to the Force. You believe it's this boy?"[57]

Later, before the same Council (this time with Anakin) Qui–Gon is distressed to discover that the Council will not train Anakin to be a Jedi. "He is the chosen one. You must see it." exclaims Qui–Gon, offering to take on Anakin at his Padawan learner. At the end of *A Phantom Menace*, Qui–Gon, with his dying words to Obi Wan, pleads "Promise me you will train the boy. He is the chose one. He will bring balance. Train him."

Early on in *Attack of the Clones*, Mace Windu counsels Obi Wan regarding Anakin, "Remember, Obi Wan, if the prophecy is true, your apprentice is the only one who can bring the Force back into balance."

This theme echoes again in *Revenge of the Sith*. As events continue to deteriorate, point to the ominous conclusion that the Sith have taken control of the Republic in a series of clandestine moves, Obi Wan Kenobi an Mace Windu discuss the uncertainty surrounding Anakin. Mace admits his thinking about him, "I don't trust him."

Perhaps hesitatingly sharing Mace's sentiments, Obi Wan asks "With all due respect, Master, is he not the chose one? Is he not to destroy the Sith and bring balance to the Force?"

"So the prophecy says." responds Mace, with a note of skepticism, if not contempt in his voice.

The Yoda injects an observation that just might warrant skepticism. "A prophecy that misread could have been."

In contrast, Christianity realizes that good and evil are not two sides of the same thing. Instead, the Christian God is absolutely good with no taint of evil or darkness:

> This is the message we have heard from him and proclaim to you, that God is light, and in him is no darkness at all. If we say we have fellowship with him while we walk in darkness, we lie and do not practice the truth. But if we walk in the light, as he is in the light, we have fellowship with one another, and the blood of Jesus his Son cleanses us from all sin. (1 John 1:5–7)

Evil arises when we use our free will to conduct ourselves contrary to the way that God has created us to be and contrary to the way that God has willed for us to act. Rather than any sort of balance between the two, Christianity realizes that someday God will relegate all evil to an eternal repository of punishment. (Matthew 7:22–23; John 5:28–29; Revelation 21:15.)

Knowledge

Star Wars embraces a method of knowing that can be characterized as anti–empirical; it disparages the value of the senses to give us reliable knowledge of reality. Obi Wan begins his training of Luke into the ways of the Force. After a few attempts to fend off with his light saber the stinging shots from the floating remote, Obi Wan increases the difficulty of the exercise by taking away Luke's advantage of sight. He says, "I suggest you try it again, Luke. This time, let go of your conscious self and act on instinct," as he is offering him a flight helmet to put on.

Luke realizes, "With the blast shield down, I can't even see. How am I supposed to fight?"

Obi Wan's answer is readily forthcoming. "Your eyes can deceive you. Don't trust them." After another stinging shot, Obi Wan coaches "Stretch out with your feelings." Willing to give it another try, Luke raises his light saber to defend himself and successfully deflects three rapid shots from the remote. Obi Wan, excited about the journey Luke is beginning, exclaims "You see? You can do it."

Luke matches Obi Wan's excitement "You know, I did feel something. I could almost see the remote."

Obi Wan's sage commentary concludes "That's good. You've taken your first step into a larger world."[58]

In contrast, Christianity realizes that our senses, while not infallible, are the faculties that God has created us with to know the creation He has made. In fact, the case for the truth of Christianity itself, especially of the resurrection in particular, is based on eyewitness testimony. (Luke 24:36–43; Acts 1:3; 1 John 1:1–2)

Reason

Throughout the movies, we see that one's interaction with the Force, and consequently the manner in which important decision are to be made, is based more on feelings rather than thinking. Revisiting Obi Wan's early training of Luke, he encouraged him to "stretch out with your feelings."[59] Qui–Gon's counsels the young Anakin before his big pod race, "Remember, concentrate on the moment. Feel, don't think. Use your instincts."[60]

When Anakin is faced with the decision whether to accept Qui–Gon's offer to go with him and become a Jedi, Anakin turns to him mother for guidance since he is understandably distraught with the prospect of leaving his mother. Her counsel is "Listen to your feelings, Annie. You know what's right."[61]

We see how Yoda trains the youngling in the ways of the Force when he says "Reach out and sense the Force. Use your feelings you must."[62] Perhaps the most amusing appeal to feelings is the refrain repeated in each of the six movies: "I have a bad feeling about this."[63]

In contrast, Christianity maintains that God is one to be discovered through creation, known by reason, and loved with one's heart. (Matt. 22:36, 37)

Hate and Anger

We see in how Yoda instructs Luke that hate and anger are always opposed to the good side. "A Jedi's strength flows from the Force. But beware of the Dark Side—anger, fear, aggression: the Dark Side of the Force are they. Easily they flow. Quick to join you in a fight. If once you start down the dark path, forever will it dominate your destiny. Consume you it will as it did Obi Wan's apprentice."[64]

In Christianity, it matters what it is that someone might hate or be angry about. Certainly hate and anger have their place, both literally and figuratively. Jesus himself said,

> Do not think that I came to bring peace on earth. I did not come to bring peace but a sword. For I have come to set a man against his father, a daughter against her mother, and a daughter–in–law against her mother–in–law and a man's enemies will be those of his own household. (Matthew 10)

To be sure, the enemies we make as Christians is not necessarily physical but, rather, is ideological. Jesus forces his disciples to make a decision about matters of truth and righteousness. Such a stand will inevitably alienate those around us, include perhaps members of our own family, to be pitted against us in their words and actions. Since Christianity is ground in truth, it is unavoidable that anyone who rejects the truth will also rejects Christ's disciples.

But even in Christianity, there is the reality of actual physical anger. As Christ's disciples, we are taught to love our enemies (Matt. 5:43–44). But this does not preclude us from defending others from the harm that evil men might exact upon them, as, for example, the Allied forces did against the Axis powers in WWII. (Jer. 22:3.) Ultimately, the day will come when Jesus Himself will execute judgment on the evil in this world and wage war against all that stands against God. (Rev. 19:11–15; 20:7–9.) When it comes to the final showdown between the forces of God and the forces of God's enemies, the last thing that is called for the Good be "beware of anger ... aggression" as Yoda would have it.

Knowing Good and Evil

Not only are important decisions managed by feelings, but *Star Wars* teaches that one's discernment between good and evil is by feelings as well. When Yoda was training Luke on Dagobah, Luke asks "Is the Dark Side stronger?"

Yoda assures him that it is not, but warns him that it is more seductive.

The next logical question in Luke's mind is "But how am I to know the good side from the bad?"

Yoda's answer is revealing. "You will know. When you are calm, at peace, passive."[65]

Such a criterion can be fatal. That is why the Bible teaches that one knows good from evil by testing, evidence, and discernment. (1 John 4:1; 1 Thess. 5:21; Hebrews 5:13–14.) It is not always an easy judgment to make. But Christianity realizes that our being "calm, at peace, passive" does not always track what is good and righteous.

Human Nature

In Star Wars, our human nature is ultimately a non–physical luminosity. While explaining the nature of the Force, Yoda pokes Luke's shoulder as if to emphasize the contrast to his physical body, "Luminous beings are we. Not the crude matter."[66]

Christianity, by contrast, teaches that humans are both physical and non–physical. (Genesis 2:7) It avoids the crass hedonism that sometimes attends the increasingly popular materialist world view, the view that all of realty is physical. But it also avoids the self–righteous asceticism or Gnosticism that denigrates the realty and goodness that attends the physical world in its attempt to live as if all that is real is non–physical. (Col. 2:16–23) This world view has to ultimate deny that God was incarnate in Jesus since, as they see it, the physical world is either non–existence or, if it has any modicum of reality, is evil in itself. Such a heresy was already manifesting itself in the Apostle John's day. (1 John 4:1–3.) Again, even if they granted some reality to the physical realm, they invariably deny that Jesus was raised physically from the dead.[67]

Life after Death

It is hard to tell specifically earlier on in *A Phantom Menace*, but the screen play makes it clear that upon death, the Jedi Knight is absorbed into the Force as in pantheism. In the fight Obi Wan Kenobi and Qui–Gon Jinn have with Darth Maul, Qui–Gon Jinn is tragically killed. With words of comfort as Qui–Gon's body goes up in flames, Obi Wan assures Anakin, "He is one with the Force, Anakin… You must let go."[68]

Later, however, this idea becomes explicit when Yoda is counseling Anakin, "Death is a natural part of life. Rejoice with those around you who transform into the Force. Mourn them do not. Miss them do not."[69] In *Return of the Jedi*, Yoda describes his immanent death as when he will "forever sleep."

That the movies convey this view of human nature can also be inferred from several lines of evidence in the movies. First, in *A New Hope* when Obi Wan decides to "give his life" for the greater good, he willingly submits to Darth Vader's light saber. But we quickly see that, upon his death Obi Wan has actually dematerialized. Later, in *Return of the Jedi* upon Luke's second visit to Dagobah, he is with Yoda when Yoda dies. Immediately upon his passing, we see Yoda's body completely disappear. The third example (essential to account for appearance of all three on the forest moon of Endor) is the hardest one to maintain as it is not as explicit as the first two.

In *Return of the Jedi*, after Luke eases Anakin (formerly Darth Vader) into his death, we see Luke dragging away what might appear as Anakin's body. It might be more reasonable (and consistent with what we have already seen) to conclude that, in fact, it was merely Darth Vader's life support suit that Luke was dragging, not Anakin's physical body. Since both Obi Wan and Yoda (as Jedi masters) dematerialized upon their deaths, and since we see all three at the end of *Return of the Jedi* appear to Luke during the celebration on the forest moon of Endor, then is it likely that Anakin also dematerialized upon his death.

Is it not surprising that this would find its way into the movies as it appears that this is Lucas's own view. He told Time magazine, "When you die, your energy field joins all other energy fields in the universe, and while you're still living that larger energy field is sympathetic to your own energy field."[70]

In stark contrast to the gnostic view of death and the afterlife conveyed in the movies, Christianity teaches that both the good and the evil retain their personal identity and are physically resurrected from the dead (John 5:28–29). The destiny of the saved is not an "eternal sleep" but rather unending life in eternal fellowship with God. (2 Cor. 5:7–8).

5 | WHAT IS THE SOURCE OF THE FORCE?

"I have a bad feeling about this."

—Han Solo, *Star Wars*

Star Wars is the religion of the Force. But what is the source of George Lucas's concept of the Force? According to Dale Pollock in *Skywalking*,

> Lucas's concept of the Force was heavily influenced by Carlos Castaneda's *Tales of Power*. This is an account of a Mexican Indian sorcerer, Don Juan, who uses the phrase "life force."[71]

Similarity with Castaneda's View

Not only does Lucas borrow the concept of the Force from Castaneda but in many cases the vocabulary is virtually identical.

- They both use the term "Force" and identify it as an "ally."[72]

- This Force has both a good and an evil side.[73]

- It is the "binding force of life."[74]

- It is "everywhere."[75]

- It is "outside the realm of reason." One must

"feel" the Force.[76]

- They both deny that man is "crude matter" or a "solid body,"[77] and claim that we are in reality "luminous beings."[78]

- Both the Jedi "Knight" and Castaneda's Yaqui "warrior" are to be calm and at peace when in control of the Force.[79]

These similarities are striking. But if Lucas admittedly got his concept of the Force from Castaneda, then the question is what is the religious source of Castaneda's ideas?

Similarities with Eastern Religions

Richard de Mille, in *The Don Juan Papers*, put together a collection of scholarly essays which argue that Castaneda is one of "the world's great hoaxer."[80] They claim Castaneda's Yaqui (Mexican) sorcerer don Juan is not only unfindable, but his "teachings bore no resemblance to a Yaqui way of knowledge."[81] Furthermore, authorities on Yaqui culture say that "don Juan's teachings contradicted what was known of Yaqui ways."[82]

Agehananda Bharati, an ordained Hindu monk in the Dashanami Sannyasi order, claims that Castaneda's books are actually made up of concepts taken from eastern religions. Bharati says "there is nothing in Castaneda's mysticism that you cannot also find, sometimes in nearly the same words, in Hindu and Buddhist tantrism [mystical writings] or in the official Patanjali yoga."[83]

Bharati insists "that all of Amerindian [American Indian] mystical and ecstatic lore, north, central, and south, compares with Hindu–Buddhist traditions about as a country choir compares with the B–Minor Mass.…" Thus "insofar as don Juan's teaching resembles these traditions it must have come from them and cannot have come from the Western hemisphere."[84]

The ultimate source of Castaneda's concept of the Force seems clearly oriental. Lucas reacted against his nominal protestant Christian background and developed his beliefs in accord with his own mystical experience and sense of divine destiny. So despite some western twists, the religion of the Force is substantially the same as that expressed in Eastern religious traditions.

The director of *The Empire Strikes Back*, Irvin Kershner, is a Zen Buddhist. His admission of religious intent in the movie is very explicit: "I wanna introduce some Zen here because I don't want the kids to walk away just feeling that everything is shoot–em–up, but that there's also a little something to think about here in terms of yourself and your surroundings."[85] Kershner even speaks of Yoda, the Jedi trainer, as a "Zen Master."

Lucas's biographer, Dale Pollock, concludes: "Yoda's philosophy is Buddhist—he tells Luke that the Force requires him to be calm, at peace, and passive; it should be used for knowledge and defense, not greed and aggression."[86] The Star Wars parallel with Eastern religion is further exemplified in the belief that "when people die, their life spirit is drained from them and incorporated in a huge energy force,"[87] joining "the ethereal oneness of the Force."[88]

So, wittingly or unwittingly, Lucas presents a dramatic portrayal of a Zen Buddhist conception of God which he calls the Force, but in Zen is known as the Tao.

Castaneda's Similarities with the Occult

Kenneth Minogue, Professor of Political Science at the University of London, unhesitatingly concludes that "Castaneda is entirely in the Occultist tradition."[89] The supporting evidence for this charge is strong:

> Professor of Philosophy at Los Angeles Pierce College and occult expert, Douglass McFerran, says that "Don Juan calls himself a brujo, a word that in rural Mexico unfailingly indicates the practitioner of a harmful magic."[90]

Professor McFerran goes on to say that "Sorcerers like don Juan and don Genaro are come ... to guide a new cycle of apprentices in a magical tradition reaching back to the days of the Indian civilization that preceded the Aztecs. In a telling phrase their disciples refer to them as 'Toltec devils.' To anyone familiar with Mesoamerican mythology this suggests the image of the Plumed Serpent, the warrior god Quetzalcoatl, whom the Spanish conquerors equated with Satan. And Quetzalcoatl, it should be remembered, was represented in Indian art as both benign and horribly malevolent."[91]

Clear evidences of paranormal behavior is indicated by such activities as men transforming themselves into various animals,[92] feats of levitation/transportation,[93] and out–of–body experiences.[94]

> **"Beware of them.**
> **A heavy price is paid**
> **for the power they bring."**
> –Yoda to Luke

On the swampy planet of Dagobah, Yoda warns Luke about the good and evil sides of the Force (which is reminiscent of the Mesoamerican god, Quetzalcoatl). Furthermore, Yoda, in paranormal fashion, levitates Luke's X–wing fighter (ESB 124) and makes an extra–sensory claim that "through the Force things you will see: other places, other thoughts, the future, the past, old friends long gone."[95]

Sanford Bergman, an authority on library cataloguing, places the works of Castaneda under the headings of "Witchcraft" and "Magic."[96] If this is so, then the Star Wars trilogy should be placed there as well.

6 | WHAT IS THE GOSPEL ACCORDING TO LUCAS?

"Open yourself to the Force you must."

—Yoda

What is the central spiritual message Lucas wished to convey in the films? It seems to be twofold. There is a moral message and a religious message. They are closely related.

The Moral Message

Lucas admits writing the film series as a "modern morality play."[97] He wants to teach values to a rootless society. Thus he wrote a timeless fable that could illustrate in a non–dogmatic way the differences between right and wrong.

The beginning—"a long time ago in a galaxy far away"—is Lucas's version of "once upon a time." He believes children understand the message. They realize that eventually they will have to leave home, undergo the trials of life, and learn to act like adults. What children do not know is how to make these decisions. Star Wars is designed to show them.[98]

More simply put, the moral message of Star Wars is that we can escape a life of monotonous routine by accept-

ing the responsibility for our decisions and their conse-
quences.[99] In Lucas's own words, "All were designed to
teach man the right way to life and give him a moral anchor."[100] Thus the moral premise of Star Wars, according to
Lucas, is that you cannot avoid making tough decisions.[101]

The Religious Message

Lucas summarized his religious message in Star Wars
in these words: "I was trying to say in a very simple way
… that there is a God and there is both a good side and a
bad side. You have a choice between them, but the world
works better if you're on the good side."[102]

In elaborating on this message Lucas believes that
even the most evil of men, like Darth Vader, have good
in them. Luke Skywalker is made to say, "There's good in
him, I've felt it.… I can save him, I can turn him back to
the good side."[103] In the end the evil Vader was converted
back to the good side of the Force when he recognized
that "there must have been good in him, too. He smiled up
again at his son, and for the first time, loved him. And for
the first time in many long years, loved himself again, as
well."[104]

There is a message of salvation in Star Wars. It is the
message of self–reliance. It is a message which says: trust
your instincts. Rely on your feelings, not your senses or
reason. Your feelings will direct you to the good side. All
men have good in them which can be activated by letting

the good side of the Force flow through them freely.[105] Patient concentration is necessary. Utter faith in the Force can move mountains. "Knowledge of the Force and how to manipulate it was what gave the Jedi his special power."[106] As Ben Kenobi told Luke, "You must learn to admit the Force when you want it, so that you can learn to control it consciously."[107]

So the way of salvation according to Lucas is the gospel of self–reliance. It is the gospel of human self–sufficiency to control the Force [God] by using it to conquer fear and aggression and to attain immortality. The gospel of Star Wars is also the gospel which proclaims that in the end even the evil Darth Vader has good in him and can be converted to the good side. According to Robert Short, it is the gospel which claims "that eventually everyone—even Darth Vader and the Devil—will thankfully serve Christ and worship him."[108]

"Only different in your mind.

You must unlearn

what you have learned."

—Yoda, *Force vs. Father*

What is the difference between the gospel according to Lucas and the gospel according to Luke? Is the religion of the Jedi the same as the religion of Jesus? Robert Short suggests that it is.[109] But we have seen that there is a vast difference between a cosmic Force and a heavenly Father; between an impersonal Power and a personal Being; between an amoral Energy and a moral Entity.

In short, the Force is not at all the same as the Christian concept of God. The Christian "God so loved the world that He gave His only Son" (John 3:16); the Force has no love for the world. God knows all His creatures and cares for them (Matt. 6:25–34). The Force has no knowledge or concern for humans; it is simply a power to be used by them.

Feeling vs. Thinking

Another difference in the religion of the Jedi and that of Jesus is this: Jesus called upon his disciples to love God with all their "heart and … mind …" (Matt. 22:37–38). His disciples were to "avoid … contradictions …" (1 Tim. 6:20) and the irrational. They were urged, "Always be prepared to make a defense to any one …" (1 Peter 3:15). They presented "many proofs" of Christ's deity (Acts 1:3). They "argued with them from the scriptures, explaining and proving that it was necessary for the Christ to suffer and to rise from the dead …" (Acts 17:2, 3).

In short, Christianity appeals to the reason as well as the heart. It is a rational belief. It bids its followers to "test the spirits to see whether they are from God" and to discern the difference between "the spirit of truth and the spirit of error" (1 John 4:1, 6).

Christianity does not bypass the head on the way to the heart. It is not a mindless belief. It says "Look before you leap." It offers satisfaction for one's soul without demanding the sacrifice of one's mind. On the other hand, the religion of the Jedi is not rational but mystical. It is not based on reason but on feeling. The Jedi cannot be successful if they trust their senses or reason.[110] It is not a religion based on fact but on feeling.

Lucas's childhood mystical experience plus the auto accident when a teenager led him to depend more and more on his feelings. He said he began to trust his instincts. When he had the feeling that he should go to college, he went to college. When he had the feeling to make Star Wars, he did, even though his friends told him he was crazy.[111]

"Forget your old measures.
Unlearn! Unlearn!"
−Yoda to Luke Skywalker

An implicit trust in feelings is a central theme of Star Wars. Luke is told "Relax! Be free. You're trying to use your eyes and ears. Stop predicting."[112]

In a moment of faith Luke exclaimed: "I feel the Force!"[113] His Jedi master, Yoda, exhorted: "There is no why…. Clear your mind of questions."[114]

For the Jedi reason is not used to tap into the power of the Force, One must transcend senses and reason; he must feel the Force. One must not be active in thinking about the Force; he must be passive in feeling it. Just relax and "let the Force flow."[115] "Open yourself to the Force you must."[116]

The belief that one must totally trust his feelings is vividly portrayed in the final scenes of Star Wars, where Luke is about to enter into the surface trench of the Death Star with his X−wing fighter. But before he gets his chance, Obi−Wan Kenobi reminds Luke to trust his feelings. Luke heeds his mentor's words and switches off his targeting computer even though he needs to make a "one−in−a−million" direct hit at exactly ninety degrees on a small, two−meter thermal exhaust port in order to destroy the whole space station. The contrast is complete here: either trust your reason (use the computer) or trust your intuition (feel the Force).

Self–Effort vs. Divine Help

There is another significant difference between the gospel according to Lucas and the gospel of Christ. For Lucas salvation is by human effort; according to Christ, salvation is by divine grace (Eph. 2:8–9). Luke Skywalker, by contrast, became a Jedi by great personal effort. It took patience[117] and great concentration to attain this status.[118]

Indeed, the Jedi master, Yoda, picked only those disciples who had the deepest commitment.[119] A Jedi was one who became completely self–reliant in his use of the Force. With great discipline and long practice he learned to use the Force. He gained total conscious control of the Force.[120] He could manipulate the Force for his own ends.[121]

By self–control one can conquer his evil tendencies including anger, fear, hatred and aggression.[122] All this is within human grasp; it is power that all men have available naturally for it is the energy that surrounds us all. Vader grew weaker and weaker after rescuing Luke from the Emperor. Luke cried out, "I've got to save you." To which Vader responded, "You already have."[123] Their efforts to overcome evil led to Vader's salvation—to be one with the Force along with Yoda and Obi–Wan.

By contrast, the gospel of Christianity declares that men are evil (Rom. 3:10–23) and that they cannot do anything to attain their own salvation. "Without me you can do nothing" (John 15:5), Jesus said. St. Paul wrote, "for by grace you have been saved through faith; and that is not of yourselves, it is the gift of God; not as a result of works, that no one should boast" (Eph. 2:8–9).

The Christian gospel is one of grace; the gospel of Star Wars is one of works. According to Lucas, man can save himself. According to Luke (the apostle of Jesus, not the Skywalker), "The Son of Man has come to seek and to save that which is lost" (Luke 19:10). In Star Wars salvation is by self–effort. In the Bible salvation is by divine deliverance. The message of Star Wars is salvation by manipulating a natural power. The message of Christianity is salvation by appropriating a supernatural Person. The two "gospels" are worlds apart.

All Winners vs. Some Losers

Not only are the two "gospels" worlds apart, but Christianity, in contrast to Star Wars, declares that in the end there are two worlds which will be apart—forever. Jesus said,

> When the Son of man comes in his glory, and all the angels with him, then he will sit on his glorious throne. Before him will be gathered all the nations, and he will separate them one from another as a shepherd separates the sheep from the goats, and he will place the sheep at his right hand, but the goats at the left. Then the King will say to those at his right hand, 'Come, O blessed of my Father, inherit the kingdom prepared for you from the foundation of the world'.... Then he will say to those at his left hand, 'Depart from me, you cursed, into the eternal fire prepared for the devil and his angels'

(Matt. 25:31–34, 41).

In other words, while the Jedi religion prophesies that evil will eventually and ultimately merge with good, [124] according to Jesus, the evil will ultimately be separated from the good. According to *The Gospel from Outer Space,* there will eventually be a great marriage of heaven and hell. But according to Christianity, the end will bring the great divorce. As the author of another famous science trilogy put it,

> There are only two kinds of people in the end: those who say to God, 'Thy will be done,' and those to whom God says, in the end. 'Thy will be done.' All that are in Hell, choose it. Without that self–choice there could be no Hell. No soul that seriously and constantly desires joy will ever miss it. Those who seek find. To those who knock it is opened.[125]

Christianity says, there is an ultimate choice to make in the deadly serious "game" of life. As in other games, some win and some lose but all must choose.

"There is a way which seems right to a man,
but its end is the way to death."
—Proverbs 14:12

Does it make any difference whether one follows the religion of the Jedi or the religion of Jesus? Do not all religions point in the same basic direction?

A Hindu Parable

Are not all the religions describing the same basic reality in different ways? Note the story of the six blind men and the elephant. [126] The blind man holding the leg of the elephant said, "This is a tree." Another grasping the trunk declared, "This is a large snake." The third blind man with the ear flapping in his face was positive it was a fan. But the one who was feeling the elephant's side pronounced, "This is a wall." The fifth blind man who had a hold on the tail was certain it was a rope. But the one who was feeling the tusk exclaimed to all, "This is a spear."

Now each blind man believed he was right and the others were wrong. But in this they were all wrong.[127] Yet in another sense they were all seem right, because one and the same elephant seemed different things to different people. And so it is, we are told, with religion. There are many ways to describe the Ultimate and how one should relate to it. Each is right in its own way, but none is right if it declares itself the only way. But is this really so? Is the elephant really six different things?

In response to this parable one can understand how six blind men could think an elephant was six different things. But reasonable persons should open their eyes and look at reality. Certainly six sighted persons would not think that the elephant was six different things! As the poet Francis Bourdillon put it,

> The night has a thousand eyes,
> And the day but one;
> Yet the light of the bright world dies
> With the dying sun.

Jesus said,

> I am the light of the world;
> he who follows me shall not walk in the darkness,
> but shall have the light of life.[128]

Contrary to the religion of the Jedi, Christianity bids men to open their eyes and think about the Christ, not to close their eyes and feel the Force.

Christianity is based on historical facts of a real person, Jesus of Nazareth, who lived, died, and rose from the dead. The Jedi religion is not based on objective facts but on subjective feelings. By contrast, Jesus asked, "What do you think about the Christ" (Matt. 22:42). The Jedi are asked: "Can you feel the Force?" Jesus challenged His disciples, "See My hands and my feet, that it is I. Touch me and see for yourselves a spirit does not have flesh and bones as you see that I have" (Luke 24:39). Christianity does not say "Close your eyes and feel the cosmic Force." It says "Open your eyes and look at the historical facts."[129]

A Hindu Guru

The basic difference was stated well by a Hindu Guru, Rabindranath R. Maharaj, in his struggle for enlightenment.

> The real conflict was between two opposing views of God: was God all that there was—or could he make a rock or a man without its being part of himself? If there

was only One Reality, then Brahman was evil as well as good, death as well as life, hatred as well as love. That made everything meaningless, life an absurdity. It was not easy to maintain both one's sanity and the view that good and evil, love and hate, life and death were One Reality.

Furthermore, if good and evil were the same, then all karma was the same and nothing mattered, so why be religious? It seemed unreasonable; but ... Reason could not be trusted—it was part of the illusion. If Reason also was maya—as the Vedas taught—then how could I trust any concept, including the idea that all was maya and only Brahman was real? How could I be sure that the Bliss I sought was not also an illusion, if none of my perceptions or reasonings were to be trusted?

To accept what my religion taught I had to deny what Reason told me. But what about other religions? If all was One, then they were all the same. That seemed to deify confusion as the Ultimate Reality.[130]

What difference does it make? It is the difference between confusion and clarity; between darkness and light; between night and day. The difference is that between "six blind Hindus" and one enlightened Guru who received light from the One who said, "I am the light of the world; he who follows me shall not walk in the darkness, but shall have the light of life" (John 8:12). In the Guru's own words,

I knew that Jesus wasn't just another one of several million gods. He was in fact the God for whom I had hungered. I had met Jesus by faith and discovered that he himself was the Creator. Yet he loved me enough to become a man for my sake and to die for my sins. With that realization, tons of darkness seemed to lift and a brilliant light flooded my–soul.[131]

Richard G. Howe earned his PhD in philosophy from the University of Arkansas. He is the Professor Emeritus of Philosophy and Apologetics at Southern Evangelical Seminary of Charlotte, NC. There he trains eager padawans on topics of philosophy, world religions, occultism, lightsabers, and more.

http://richardghowe.com

http://SES.edu

Norman L. Geisler has authored or co-authored more than ninety books. He earned his PhD in philosophy from Loyola University. He is the Chancellor and Distinguished Professor of Theology and Apologetics at Veritas Evangelical Seminary. He is also the Distinguished Senior Professor of Theology and Apologetics at Southern Evangelical Seminary. He has authored or co-authored over 100 books which have sold over one million copies.

http://NormGeisler.com

http://BastionBooks.com

http://VES.edu

We can Know

Can a creature really know its Creator? Perhaps at first this seems like asking whether or not a dab of paint on a canvas can know its Painter and whether a pinch of clay in a sculpture can know its Potter. But we humans are very different than paint and clay; we were born to wonder, learn, ponder, and know.

It makes no sense to say "we can't know anything about anything about reality" or "we can't know anything about God." This is the same as saying, "I know with certainty that the only thing that we can know with certainty is that we cannot know anything with certainty." No matter how we approach it, it is possible to know something about reality.

Creation implies Creator

We know that if our world had a beginning it must also have had a Beginner. If it was created, it was created by a Creator, for nothing cannot produce something. From the fact of creation we know that our Creator possesses an unfathomable amount of power. We also know that he is not an impersonal force; he is a being that made a conscious choice between creating and not creating.

Design implies Designer

The more we learn about our amazing universe, the more overwhelmingly clear it becomes that everything was designed with exquisite care. Wherever we look—our galaxy cluster, the arms of our spiral galaxy, solar system, planet Earth, the living cells in us, the complex information encoded into the double-helix, atoms, and the sub-atomic realm—we see fine-tuning that could have only been accomplished by a superlatively intelligent, purposeful Designer. It requires a tremendous amount of blind faith to conclude that we and our world are somehow the result of random, accidental, chaotic, mindless, unthinking, uncaring, purposeless happenstance. We can know that our Creator is an Artist and Architect.

Only a Mind can create minds

Clearly we were created as persons; we think, make choices, communicate, feel, and care. The fact that we were endowed with these abilities is a proof that our Creator is also a personal Being. Causes cannot give to their effects what they themselves do not have to give. The impersonal and mindless forces that govern our world could not invent us if they would, nor would they if they could. It's more reasonable to believe that a great Mind created minds than to think that non-mind could or would create either minds or matter. As we begin to realize that it takes a personal being to choose to create our world and beings like us, the tantalizing possibility arises that we can go beyond merely knowing about God and into knowing God in a person-to-person kind of relationship!

He has not been silent

Some may insist that God must be too holy, good, big, different, spiritual, and transcendent to communicate with little beings like us. And, if so, we cannot successfully reach out to him. But what if God decided to reach out to us? What if he took the initiative to break the silence and make himself known to us in some way? Surely if he wanted to he could find one or more ways to communicate some truths about himself to us. Others might object that we live in a "closed universe," which God cannot reach into, speak into, or even affect indirectly. However, the one who is great enough to create a world can reach into it. And the Mind that created our minds can find a way to communicate with us if he pleases.

Over the last few thousand years, hundreds of men and women have claimed that they have heard from God and that they speak for him. It's an easy claim to make. But it's not an easy claim to substantiate. Very few prophets had their claims authenticated by something unequivocally supernatural. We can know a prophet speaks for God if he or she exhibits a clear knowledge of the future (that only God could know) or performs miraculous acts (that only God's power could perform). The Bible is a collection of books written by prophets and apostles who were authenticated in these ways. One prophet who predicted the future in flawless detail many times also told us that knowing God is both possible and valuable:

> Thus says the Lord: "Let not the wise man boast in his wisdom, let not the mighty man boast in his might, let not the rich man boast in his riches, but let him who boasts boast in this, that he understands and knows me, that I am the Lord who practices steadfast love, justice, and righteousness in the earth. For in these things I delight, declares the Lord." (Jeremiah 9:23–24)

Paul, another one of God's messengers who was authenticated by miraculous signs (2 Corinthians 12:12), indicated that God did leave some clues for us to find. The rain and sunshine that produces the food we enjoy every day is evidence that God cares about us.

> . . . you should turn from these vain things [idols] to a living God, who made the heaven and the earth and the sea and all that is in them. In past generations he allowed all the nations to walk in their own ways. Yet he did not leave himself without witness, for he did good by giving you rains from heaven and fruitful seasons, satisfying your hearts with food and gladness. (Acts 14:15–17)

Why we don't know

Paul also said that we should already know several things about God by considering the world he created. The problem is not that God's fingerprints are not left all over creation; the problem is that we tend to suppress that knowledge. We replace the infinite God with finite things. We swap the uncreated Creator with the creatures. Instead of seeking God and thanking God, we all naturally turn away from him and try to forget him.

> For what can be known about God is plain to them, because God has shown it to them. For his invisible attributes, namely, his eternal power and divine nature, have been clearly perceived, ever since the creation of the world, in the things that have been made. So they are without excuse. For although they knew God, they did not honor him as God or give thanks to him, but they became futile in their thinking, and their foolish hearts were darkened. Claiming to be wise, they became fools, and exchanged the glory of the immortal God for images resembling mortal man and birds and animals and creeping things. (Romans 1:19–21)

Seek and find

We encourage you to take the first step towards knowing God. Turn your heart and mind towards him and begin seeking him diligently.

> You will seek me and find me, when you seek me with all your heart. I will be found by you, declares the LORD. (Jeremiah 29:13)

> And he made from one man every nation of mankind. . . that they should seek God, in the hope that they might feel their way toward him and find him. Yet he is actually not far from each one of us. (Acts 17:26–27)

> Anyone who comes to him must believe that he exists and that he rewards those who earnestly seek him. (Hebrews 11:6)

The problem of sin

As we begin a sincere search for God, we realize there is more than just a great distance between us. The moral obstacle of sin looms large. We need forgiveness of our sins before we can begin to enjoy a friendly relationship with God.

> Behold, the days are coming. . . when I will be their God, and they shall be my people. And no longer shall each one teach his neighbor and each his brother, saying, "Know the LORD," for they shall all know me, from the least of them to the greatest, declares the LORD. For I will forgive their iniquity, and I will remember their sin no more. (Jeremiah 31:31–34)

This dilemma should not surprise us. From the sense of right and wrong inside us all, we can and should know that our Creator is concerned about the decisions we make. God is the moral Being who created us as moral beings. He is the one who encoded that intuitive sense of "treat others as you would have them treat you" deeply into us. Knowing that he sets standards for righteousness and justice, we can expect that he cares about those standards. Since we know that we have not always done and said what we know we should have, we can also suspect that we need mercy and forgiveness from God.

Before we can begin to enjoy a friendly relationship with God, we need to come to terms with the fact that from God's standpoint we are enemies, sinners, strangers, and exiles. We are not good.

No one is righteous, no, not one; no one understands; no one seeks for God. All have turned aside; together they have become worthless; no one does good, not even one. (Romans 3:10–12)

The solution

The good news is that God already opened the door to reconciliation, forgiveness, and the possibility of beginning a personal relationship with him!

. . . while we were God's enemies, we were reconciled to him through the death of his Son. (Romans 5:10)

. . . in Christ God was reconciling the world to himself, not counting their trespasses against them. . . . We implore you on behalf of Christ, be reconciled to God. For our sake he made him to be sin who knew no sin, so that in him we might become the righteousness of God. (2 Corinthians 5:18–21)

There is now no condemnation for those who are in Christ Jesus. (Romans 8:1)

I now consider loss for the sake of Christ. What is more, I consider everything a loss compared to the surpassing greatness of knowing Christ Jesus my Lord, for whose sake I have lost all things. I consider them rubbish, that I may gain Christ and be found in him, not having a righteousness of my own that comes from [obeying] the law, but that which is through faith in Christ—the righteousness that comes from God and is by faith. I want to know Christ and the power of his resurrection. (Philippians 3:7–11)

Knowing God by knowing Jesus

God made himself known to us not just by leaving a witness for us to ponder, and not just by speaking to and through a few prophets and apostles. He made himself known to us by sending his Son to become one of us!

> Long ago, at many times and in many ways, God spoke to our fathers by the prophets, but in these last days he has spoken to us by his Son, whom he appointed the heir of all things, through whom also he created the world. He is the radiance of the glory of God and the exact imprint of his nature, and he upholds the universe by the word of his power. (Hebrews 1:1–3)

> Jesus said to him, "I am the way, and the truth, and the life. No one comes to the Father except through me. If you had known me, you would have known my Father also. From now on you do know him and have seen him." Philip said to him, "Lord, show us the Father, and it is enough for us." Jesus said to him, "Have I been with you so long, and you still do not know me, Philip? **Whoever has seen me has seen the Father**. How can you say, 'Show us the Father'? Do you not believe that I am in the Father and the Father is in me? The words that I say to you I do not speak on my own authority, but the Father who dwells in me does his works [miracles]. Believe me that I am in the Father and the Father is in me, or else believe on account of the works themselves. . . Judas (not Iscariot) said to him, "Lord, how is it that you will manifest [make known] yourself to us, and not to the world?" Jesus answered him, "If anyone loves me, he will keep my word, and my Father will love him, and we will come to him and make our home with him.

> (John 14:6–11, 22–23, emphasis added)

Accept the free gift

Some might expect that if our lack of righteousness is the problem, the way to remove the obstacle of sin is to try harder to become righteous. We naturally think that if we can just stop doing some of the bad things we do and start doing more good that somehow this attempt to "clean up our act" will make us more acceptable to God. But only God can make us truly clean; only God can deal with the problem of sin. Taking our sin from us, God offers us righteousness and his forgiveness as free gifts!

> But now the righteousness of God has been manifested. . . the righteousness of God through faith in Jesus Christ for all who believe. For. . . all have sinned and fall short of the glory of God, and are justified [declared righteous] by his grace [generosity] as a gift, through the redemption [setting free from slavery] that is in Christ Jesus, whom God put forward as a propitiation [satisfaction] by his blood, to be received by faith. This was to show God's righteousness, because in his divine forbearance he had passed over former sins. It was to show his righteousness at the present time, so that he might be just and the justifier of the one who has faith in Jesus. Then what becomes of our boasting? It is excluded.
>
> (Romans 3:21–27)

To begin to know God personally, the only thing you need to do is to humbly accept this free gift with an empty hand and a trusting heart. Simply thank Him for his generosity, mercy, and love. Gifts cannot be earned; they can only be accepted or rejected.

The wages of sin are death, but the gift of God is eternal
life in Christ Jesus our Lord. (Romans 6:23)

For by grace you have been saved through faith. And
this is not of your own doing; it is the gift of God, not
a result of works, that no one may boast. (Ephesians
2:8–9)

Accept Jesus

We accept the free gifts of righteousness, forgiveness,
and adoption by accepting Jesus. We accept Jesus by believing in him. We encourage you to trust him and wel-
come him.

But to all who did receive him [Jesus], who believed in
his name, he gave the right to become children of God.
(John 1:12)

Talk to God

Whoever shall call on the name of the Lord will be
saved. (Romans 10:13)

Personal relationships involve communication. God
has already broken the silence and reached out to us. We
urge you to turn your heart towards him and talk to him.
Consider praying along the following lines, but in your
own words:

Dear God,

*I know you created this world and have made us in
your image. But we have sinned and rebelled against
you. In spite of this, you loved each one of us—even*

me. You sent your Son to die for my sins. You raised him from the dead and will raise me from the dead someday too. I hereby repent of my sins and trust Christ alone for my righteousness, forgiveness, and salvation. Thank you for your great gifts. I thank you in Jesus' name.

Now please help me to know your better. And please teach me from your word, guide me in your work, and help me to walk in your way.

In Jesus' name, Amen.

Growing in the Knowledge of God

Peter urges those of us who have begun to know God to "grow in the grace and knowledge of our Lord and Savior Jesus Christ." The main way to know more about Jesus is the reading the Bible. But the Bible must be studied carefully and we must be wary of those who "twist" the Scriptures.

> There are some things in [Paul's letters] that are hard to understand, which the ignorant and unstable twist to their own destruction, as they do the other Scriptures. . . But grow in the grace and knowledge of our Lord and Savior Jesus Christ. To him be the glory both now and to the day of eternity. (2 Peter 3:14–18)

So it is important to find Bible teachers who shed light upon the Bible while letting it speak for itself rather than imposing a foreign meaning upon them. It is also vitally important to be connected with a community of solid, growing Christians who live by God's Word.

> And let us consider how to stir up one another to love
> and good works, not neglecting to meet together, as is
> the habit of some, but encouraging one another. (He-
> brews 10:24–25)

While it is usually easy to find church buildings, it is
not always easy to find a church that is filled with people
who have found peace with God through Christ and are
eager to grow in the grace and knowledge of him. Look
for a church that is alive and teaches the Bible as the Word
of God.

Baptism

The idea of being baptized in water may seem a little
strange at first. But it is something Christ commanded us to
do (Mt. 28:18-20). So, after you find a good Bible-teach-
ing church, ask one of the spiritual leaders how you can be
baptized.

To be clear, baptism does not save you. It is a work
of righteousness (Mt. 3:15) and we are not saved by per-
forming "works of righteousness" (Titus 3:5). We are only
saved by the graciousness of God. We are saved through
the gospel (Rom. 1:16) and baptism is not part of the gospel (1 Cor. 1:17). We are saved through faith alone (Rom.
4:5), not by any action or ritual.

Water baptism is a public testimony that you have
been buried with Christ and have risen with Him to walk

in the newness of life (Rom. 6:3-4). It is a sign to others. It's a bit like the person who gets married and begins wearing a wedding ring to inform others about that personal relationship. Similarly, baptism is a visible symbol of the relationship you have begun with God.

Additional Resources

A great first step in your new spiritual life is to read the Gospel of John. It is the fourth book in the New Testament of the Bible. It was written by one of Jesus' apostles so that you ". . . may believe that Jesus is the Christ, the Son of God, and that by believing you may have life in his name" (John 20:31).

To help you think through the tough questions about God, Jesus, and the Bible, consider these books that have helped thousands:

Twelve Points that Shows Christianity is True
by Norman Geisler (Bastion Books: 2012)

I Don't Have Enough Faith to be an Atheist
by Geisler and Turek (Crossway: 2004)

A Popular Survey of Bible Doctrine
by Geisler and Potter (Bastion Books: 2015)

For advanced studies consider:

The Big Book of Christian Apologetics
by Norman Geisler (Baker: 2012)

Systematic Theology: In One Volume
by Norman Geisler (Bethany House: 2011)

1. We say that the Force best fits a conceptual model of God that is "mostly pantheistic" (in which all that is real is part of God) because many of the truth claims about the Force fit the pantheistic model well. One clear example of this can be heard when Obi Wan explained that the Force is, "an energy field created by all living things. It surrounds us, penetrates us. It binds the galaxy together." This fits the pantheistic and panentheistic models of God well. But we also recognize that George Lucas and his saga are highly syncretistic and not every claim about the Force fits one single model. Other religio–philosophical claims about the Force in Star Wars seem to have been influenced by elements from Zoroastrian dualism, Manichean dualism, Taoism, Qigong, Prana, Zen Buddhism, and Stoicism. With some exceptions, many of these elements fit very naturally with pantheism. To learn more about the different models of God, see Norman Geisler's book *A Handbook on World Views: A Catalogue for World View Shoppers* (Bastion Books: 2013).

2. Stephen Zito, "George Lucas Goes Far Out" in Sally Kline, ed. *George Lucas Interviews* (Jackson: University of Mississippi Press, 1999), 49.

3. *Los Angeles Times*, Oct. 31, 2012 available at http://articles.latimes.com/2012/oct/31/business/la–fi–ct–disney–lucasfilm–20121101, accessed 06/29/15.

4. Industrial Light & Magic web site at http://www.ilm.com, accessed 06/29/15.

5. *Ibid.*

6. "George Lucas on Mentors and Faith." A partial transcript available at http://billmoyers.com/2012/08/09/moyers–moment–1999–george–lucas–on–mentors–and–faith as well as in Bill Moyers and George Lucas, "Of Myth and Men: A Conversation between Bill Moyers and George Lucas on the Meaning of the Force and the True Theology of *Star Wars*," in *Time*, April 26 1999. https://youtu.be/jriIX-NrN5aw accessed July 1, 2015.

7. *Ibid.*

8. *Star Wars Episode IV: A New Hope*, directed by George Lucas (1977; Burbank, CA: Twentieth Century Fox Home Entertainment), DVD. Also see George Lucas, *Star Wars* (SW), New York: Ballantine Books, 1976. 37.

9. *Ibid.*

10. *Ibid.*

11. *Ibid.*

12. "George Lucas on Mentors and Faith."

13. *Ibid.*

14. *Ibid.*

15. *Ibid.*

16. George Lucas, *Star Wars* (SW), New York: Ballantine Books, 1976. 120

17. *Star Wars Episode IV: A New Hope*, directed by George Lucas (1977; Burbank, CA: Twentieth Century Fox Home Entertainment), DVD.

18. *Star Wars Episode V: The Empire Strikes Back*, directed by Irvin Kershner (1980; Beverly Hills, CA: Twentieth Century Fox Home Entertainment), DVD.

19. "George Lucas on Mentors and Faith."

20. Bill Moyers and George Lucas, "Of Myth and Men: A Conversation between Bill Moyers and George Lucas on the Meaning of the Force and the True Theology of *Star Wars*," in *Time*, April 26 1999, 93.

21. "George Lucas on Mentors and Faith."

22. *Ibid.*

23. *Ibid.*

24. *Star Wars Episode V: The Empire Strikes Back*, directed by Irvin Kershner (1980; Beverly Hills, CA: Twentieth Century Fox Home Entertainment), DVD.

25. *Star Wars Episode III: Revenge of the Sith*, directed by George Lucas (2005; Beverly Hills, CA: Twentieth Century Fox Home Entertainment), DVD.

26. *Star Wars Episode VI: Return of the Jedi*, directed by Richard Marquand (1983; Beverly Hills, CA: Twentieth Century Fox Home Entertainment), DVD.

27. *Star Wars Episode V: The Empire Strikes Back*, directed by Irvin Kershner (1980; Beverly Hills, CA: Twentieth Century Fox Home Entertainment), DVD.

28. *Star Wars Episode I: The Phantom Menace*, directed by George Lucas (1999; Beverly Hills, CA: Twentieth Century Fox Home

Entertainment), DVD.

29. *Ibid.*

30. SKW. Dale Pollok, *Skywalking: The Life and Films of George Lucas.* (New York: Harmony Books, 1983), 139.

31. SKW 20

32. SKW 268

33. SKW 19–20

34. SKW 141

35. SKW xvi

36. SKW 3

37. *Time* (May 23, 1983), p. 68.

38. *Dallas Times Herald.* May 28, 1983. F–11

39. *Dallas Times Herald.* May 25, 1983. F–11.

40. SKW 143

41. SKW 144

42. SKW 139

43. *Newsweek* (January 1, 1979), p. 50.

44. *Dallas Morning News* (June 11, 1983), p. 55 A.

45. Robert Short, *The Gospel from Outer Space* (GS), San Francisco: Harper & Row Publishers, 1983, p. 51.

46. "George Lucas on Mentors and Faith."

47. *Book of Ritual*, 7.2.19.

48. *Sutta Nipata* 262.

49. Rom. 2:14–15 NKJV. For a discussion of how there is a Natural Law or common morality see, Norman Geisler and Frank Turek *Legislating Morality: Is it Wise? Is it Legal? Is it Possible?* (Eugene: Wipf and Stock, 1998); and J. Budziszewski, *Written on the Heart: The Case for Natural Law* (Downers Grove: InterVarsity, 1997). For a treatment of Natural Law particularly within evangelical thinking see, Jesse Covington, Bryan McGraw, and Micah Watson, eds. *Natural Law and Evangelical Political Thought* (Lanham: Lexington Books, 2013).

50. For a treatment of the world's religions see, Winfried Corduan, *Neighboring Faiths: A Christian Introduction to World Religions*, 2nd ed. (Downers Grove: InterVarsity, 2012).

51. Some might suggest that the role that the midi–chlorians (who are a life form) play vis–à–vis the Force shows that the Force is not an impersonal energy. Even Qui–Gon suggested to the Jedi Council that Anakin's conception "was the will of the Force." Two things might be said in response. First, it is possible that the movies are not internally consistent and that an argument can be sustained from episodes IV–VI that indeed the Force was depicted as an impersonal, almost pantheistic energy despite the seeming change in *A Phantom Menace*. Second, even allowing the role that the midi–chlorians play, they as life forms are still to be distinguished from the Force itself. After all, Lucas never talked about the prospect that any viewer would consider that the midi–chlorians were God, as he suspected that some viewers would regarding the Force. The midi–chlorians seem to be mere go–betweens of the Force and humans who enable humans to utilize and discern the "will" of the Force; taking 'will' as a figure of speech not unlike the way we talk about inanimate forces of nature today having wills.

52. *Star Wars Episode IV: A New Hope*, directed by George Lucas (1977; Burbank, CA: Twentieth Century Fox Home Entertainment), DVD.

53. *Star Wars Episode V: The Empire Strikes Back*, directed by Irvin Kershner (1980; Beverly Hills, CA: Twentieth Century Fox Home Entertainment), DVD.

54. *Ibid.*

55. While the notion of yin yang and balance is far eastern in origin and were incorporated later into post–Confucius Confucianism, religious Taoism, and Chinese Popular Religion, a common expression of the doctrine in the West is in Witchcraft. For example, Janet and Stewart Farrar, in their *A Witches Bible Compleat* [sic], state "The individuality is bisexual—which does not mean sexless but signifies that it contains the creative male and female essences, in dynamic balance. … Each of us has to experience both male and female incarnations, learning the lessons of each polarity, so that the dynamic balance of the Individuality may become fully developed. The concept is perfectly expressed by the Chinese Yin–Yang symbol. The white part represents the makle, positive, light, fertilizing Yang aspect …. The black part represents the female, receptive, dark, formative Yin aspects. [Janet and Steward Farrar, *The Witches Bible Compleat* (New York: Magickal Childe, 1984), 116. For more see, Winfried Corduan, *Neighboring Faiths: A Christian Introduction to World Religions*, 2 ed. (Downers Grove: InterVarsity, 2012), 392–394.

56. Winfried Corduan, *Neighboring Faiths: A Christian Introduction to World Religions*, 2 ed. (Downers Grove: InterVarsity, 2012),

392.

57. *Star Wars Episode I: The Phantom Menace Illustrated Screenplay* (New York: Ballentine, 1999), 140.

58. *Star Wars Episode IV: A New Hope*, directed by George Lucas (1977; Burbank, CA: Twentieth Century Fox Home Entertainment), DVD.

59. *Ibid.*

60. *Star Wars Episode I: The Phantom Menace Illustrated Screenplay* (New York: Ballentine, 1999), 140.

61. *Ibid.*

62. *Ibid.*

63. Obi Wan in *A Phantom Menace*; Anakin in *Attack of the Clones*; Obi Wan in *Revenge of the Sith*; Luke and Han in *A New Hope*; Leia in *The Empire Strikes Back*; C–3PO and Han in *Return of the Jedi* (Han's is a "really" bad feeling.)

64. *Star Wars Episode V: The Empire Strikes Back*, directed by Irvin Kershner (1980; Beverly Hills, CA: Twentieth Century Fox Home Entertainment), DVD.

65. *Ibid.*

66. *Ibid.*

67. For a defense of the doctrine of the physical resurrection of Jesus see, Norman L. Geisler, *The Battle for the Resurrection* (Bastion Books, 2015).

68. George Lucas, *Star Wars Episode I: The Phantom Menace Illustrated Screenplay* (New York: Ballentine, 1999), 140.

69. *Star Wars Episode III: Revenge of the Sith*, directed by George Lucas (2005; Beverly Hills, CA: Twentieth Century Fox Home Entertainment), DVD.

70. *Time* (May 19, 1980), p. 73.

71. SKW 140

72. ESB. Empire Strikes Back. 123; cf. TOP 39, 83

73. Carlos Castaneda, *Tales of Power* (TOP), New York: Pocket Books, 1974. ESB 191; RJ 138; cf. TOP 93, 284

74. ESB. Donald F. Glut, *The Empire Strikes Back*, based on a story by George Lucas, New York: Ballantine Books, 1980. 123; cf. TOP. Carlos Castaneda, *Tales of Power*, New York: Pocket Books,

1974. 132

75. SW 120; ESB 124; cf. TOP 84

76. ESB 120, 134; cf. TOP 32; 244

77. ESB 123; cf. TOP 95

78. ESB 123; cf. TOP 9

79. ESB 134–5; cf. TOP 24

80. Richard de Mille (ed.), *The Don Juan Papers (DJP)*, Santa Barbara, CA: Ross–Erickson Publishers, 1980. DJP 10

81. DJP 259

82. DJP 260

83. DJP 148

84. DJP 148–9

85. *Rolling Stone Magazine* (July 24, 1980), p. 37.

86. SKW 140

87. SKW 140

88. James Kahn, *Return of the Jedi (RJ)*, based on a story by George Lucas, New York: Ballantine Books, 1983. 204

89. DJP 185

90. DJP 251

91. DJP 252

92. Carlos Castaneda, *The Teachings of Don Juan* (TDJ), Berkeley, CA: University of California Press, 1968. TDJ 2, 32, 136–8

93. TOP 41

94. TOP 62

95. ESB 154

96. DJP 102

97. *Dallas Times Herald* (May 25, 1983), p. F–11.

98. SKW 139

99. SKW 57

100. *Ibid.*

101. SKW 138

102. *Time* (May 23, 1983), p. 68.

103. RJ 138

104. RJ 203

105. RJ 203

106. SW 81

107. SW 122

108. Robert Short, *The Gospel from Outer Space* (GS), San Francisco: Harper & Row Publishers, 1983. 55

109. GS 51

110. SW 123

111. SKW xvi

112. SW 123

113. ESB 134

114. ESB 135

115. ESB 19

116. ESB 133

117. ESB 110

118. ESB 133

119. SKW 210

120. SW 122

121. SW 81

122. ESB 134, 192

123. RJ 209

124. GS 55

125. C.S. Lewis, *The Great Divorce*. Harper Collins: 2009.

126. The parable of the blind men and the elephant can be found in the writings of Hindu, Jianist, Buddhist, and Sufi–Muslim traditions.

127. As the famous poetic rendition of this parable put it,

> *And so these men of Indostan*
> *Disputed loud and long,*
> *Exceedingly stiff and strong,*
> *Though each was partly in the right,*
> *And all were in the wrong!*

John Godfrey Saxe, *The Poems of John Godfrey Saxe*. Boston: James R. Osgood and Company, (1873) 77–78.

128. John 8:12

129. See John W. Montgomery, *History and Christianity,* San Bernadino, CA: Here's Life Publishers, Inc., 1983.

130. Rabindranath R. Maharaj, with Dave Hunt, *Death of a Guru,* Nashville: Holman Bible Publishers, 1977, p. 104.

131. Ibid., p. 137.

Printed in Great Britain
by Amazon